THE LITTLE GUIDE TO
BETTY WHITE

Published by OH!
20 Mortimer Street
London W1T 3JW

ISBN 978-1-80069-155-1

Compiled by: Lisa Dyer
Editorial: Victoria Godden
Project manager: Russell Porter
Design: Tony Seddon
Production: Freencky Portas

A CIP catalogue for this book is available from the British Library

Printed in China

10 9 8 7 6 5 4 3 2 1

THE LITTLE GUIDE TO
BETTY WHITE

Everybody needs a passion

CONTENTS

INTRODUCTION

A beloved cultural icon, the First Lady of Television, Betty White is a consummate entertainer who has achieved many landmarks in her career—from the first woman to produce her own sitcom to the oldest person to receive an Emmy. Her wisecracking banter, sharply delivered one-liners, and kind heart have earned her a cult following and legendary status, inside Hollywood and out.

Born January 17, 1922, Betty landed the lead in her school play at Beverly Hills High School, before interrupting a fledgling acting career to join the American Women's Voluntary Services during World War II, delivering supplies via PX truck through the Hollywood Hills. A move into radio led to her hosting her own show, *The Betty White Show*, but it was the co-host spot with Al Jarvis on *Hollywood on Television* where she honed her talent for live TV comedy, even performing her own live commercials – up to 58 in one day!

Sitcoms, game shows, and films followed. She created, produced, and starred in *Life with Elizabeth* and appeared as a panelist on numerous TV game shows, including *Password*, where she met her husband, the host Allen Ludden, before landing her breakout role as the man-hungry Sue Ann Nivens in *The Mary Tyler Moore Show*. She followed with star turns as the naïve ditz Rose Nylund in *The Golden Girls* and the sassy Elka Ostrovsky in *Hot in Cleveland*. In addition to countless guest appearances on everything from *The Love Boat* to *The Bold and the Beautiful*, she became endeared to a new generation of viewers through her scene-stealing roles in *Lake Placid* and *The Proposal*.

She says there's a little of Betty in all of her characters, and like many of them, she's a feisty optimist who has provided endless hilarity and feel-good moments to millions of viewers over the years. On the following pages you will find her words of wisdom in Life Lessons, quips and comebacks in Laughing Out Loud, and quotes about the acting industry in Show Business. She talks sex in Women & Romance and expresses her fondness for animals in Cats, Dogs . . . & Elephants. In Aging (Dis)Gracefully, she addresses the passing years and her immense gratitude for her long career.

Enjoy a lifetime of laughs here from Betty . . . Like her, they are pure gold.

·····································

CHAPTER
ONE

LIFE LESSONS

With sage advice on everything from stage fright to friendships, Betty offers up her optimistic outlook on life—and how important it is to always find the fun.

If one has no sense of
humor, one is in trouble.

If You Ask Me (And of Course You Won't), 2011

I know unless I'm true to
myself I couldn't be happy.
Too much emphasis is placed
today on externals and too
little on character.

AZQuotes.com

66

Keep the other person's wellbeing in mind when you feel an attack of soul-purging truth coming on.

99

Betty White in Person, 1987

> **"**
> There is rarely, if ever, a winner
> in any heated verbal exchange.
> No one's opinion is altered,
> probably only reinforced . . . and
> so much more is dredged up
> than the issue of the moment.
> **"**

Betty White in Person, 1987

"

Oh, I don't much believe in meantime. Life happens in real-time.

"

As Caroline Thomas in *The Lost Valentine*, 2011

66
Sometimes life just isn't fair, kiddo.

99

As Rose Nylund in *The Golden Girls*,
Season 3, Episode 1

Stage fright is not a show business exclusive . . . we just abuse the privilege. It is there for everyone who walks into a new job, a new date, new in-laws . . .

Betty White in Person, 1987

Keep busy and don't focus everything on you, that wears off pretty fast. It's not hard to find things you're interested in but enjoy them and indulge them.

To Katie Couric, Yahoo! News,
January 17, 2017

> **"**
> There's no formula. Keep busy with your work and your life. You can't become a professional mourner. It doesn't help you or others. Replay the good times. Be grateful for the years you had.
> **"**

On grief, in TimeGoesBy.net interview,
June 30, 2011

Third Time's the Charm

Betty's been married three times: First to Dick Barker, for less than a year, then to agent Lane Allen for two years, and last to the love of her life, game-show host Allen Ludden, who died in 1981.

Everybody needs a passion. That's what keeps life interesting. If you live without passion, you can go through life without leaving any footprints.

If You Ask Me (And of Course You Won't), 2011

That is the most comforting thing . . . I'm not looking forward to death; it's important to live while we are here. But those who have died, my mother said, now they know the secret. And someday we all will.

On death, in TimeGoesBy.net interview, June 30, 2011

You don't say the hurtful thing
even if you're irritated or upset,
because that sticks around,
or that just chips off a little of
the other guy's self-esteem.

Today with Al Roker, NBC,
November 24, 2016

Anger tears me up inside. My own . . . or anyone else's.

Betty White in Person, 1987

I'm a big cockeyed optimist. I try to accentuate the positive as opposed to the negative.

IMDb.com

I don't understand how people can get so anti-something. Mind your own business, take care of your affairs, and don't worry about other people so much.

Parade magazine, October 31, 2010

A lot of people think this is a goodie two-shoes talking. But we do have a tendency to complain rather than celebrating who we are . . . it's better to appreciate what's happening. I think we kind of talk ourselves into the negative sometimes.

ABC News, May 24, 2011

"

You're never too old for anything.

"

Sunday Morning with Katie Couric,
CBS, June 4, 2012

I just make it my business to get along with people so I can have fun. It's that simple.

IMDb.com

Friendship takes time and energy if it's going to work. You can luck into something great, but it doesn't last if you don't give it proper appreciation.

If You Ask Me (And of Course You Won't), 2011

Famous Friends

While it may be no surprise Betty was best friends with Lucille Ball, she was also close to Liberace, Mary Tyler Moore, Doris Day, and the author John Steinbeck.

"

Friendship can be so comfortable but nurture it. Don't take it for granted.

"

If You Ask Me (And of Course You Won't), 2011

It's your outlook on life that counts. If you take yourself lightly and don't take yourself too seriously, pretty soon you can find the humor in our everyday lives. And sometimes it can be a lifesaver.

Chicago Tribune, May 4, 2011

You can lie to others—not
that I would—but you cannot
lie to yourself.

People magazine, January 16, 2021

I was blessed with a mother and father who said [to] taste the good stuff now and realize how fortunate and how wonderful things are this minute because enough minutes are not wonderful that you have to save up all the good ones to make it balance out.

Daily Actor, April 24, 2012

My mother also taught me that if you lie to anybody on the planet, don't lie to that person reflected in the mirror. Always be able to meet your own eyes and know that you're telling the truth.

National Public Radio, May 8, 2011

I am interested in a lot of things—not just show business and my passion for animals. I try to keep current in what's going on in the world.

ABC News, May 24, 2011

66

I really don't care with
whom you sleep, I just care
what kind of a decent
human being you are.

99

Huffington Post, June 12, 2012

66

You don't luck into
integrity, you work at it.

99

If You Ask Me (And of Course You Won't), 2011

66

Don't let your mouth or your pen mumble.

99

Betty White in Person, 1987

"

Humans are the only ones who think it's their duty to care for children their entire lives. We're also the only species who use corn holders that look like corn on the cob when we eat corn on the cob.

"

As Rose Nylund in *The Golden Girls*, Season 5, Episode 10

Grandmothers love to give their stuff to their grandchildren. It makes us feel like we'll still be part of your lives even after we're gone.

As Grandma Annie in *The Proposal*, 2009

CHAPTER
TWO

LAUGHING OUT LOUD

In real life, as well as on screen, Betty is a quick wit with expert comedic timing. Here are some of her most memorable lines, scripted and unscripted.

Get at least eight hours of beauty sleep, nine if you're ugly.

The Late Show with David Letterman,
June 13, 2011

I think I need a new menu. Mine seems to be full of mistakes. For example, it says a small glass of tomato juice is $6.

As Rose Nylund in *The Golden Girls*, Season 5, Episode 1

I'm probably the most patient
person you know. Go ahead.
Try to think of somebody
else. I'll wait.

As Rose Nylund in *The Golden Girls*,
Season 4, Episode 13

66

I'm not one to blow my own vertubenflugen.

99

As Rose Nylund in *The Golden Girls*,
Season 2, Episode 19

I can't stay mad at my best friends. After all, we've eaten over 500 cheesecakes together.

As Rose Nylund in *The Golden Girls*, Season 4, Episode 4

All Gold

Of the four Golden Girls, Betty was the oldest cast member and the last surviving. Her character, Rose Nylund, appeared on four different TV series: *The Golden Palace* (1992), *The Golden Girls* (1985), *Nurses* (1991), and *Empty Nest* (1988).

I'm wearing a put-together from a little shop that I favor called The Back of My Closet.

Remarks at the 63rd Primetime Emmy Awards, September 18, 2011

I not only knew Houdini, but we had a very lovely relationship . . . I really thought we had something going, and then the son of a gun disappeared.

The Late Late Show with Craig Ferguson,
March 25, 2014

(Betty was four years old when Houdini died in 1926.)

"

I have the backbone of an eel.

"

IMDb.com

The best way to earn a quick buck is a 'slip-and-fall' lawsuit.

The Late Show with David Letterman,
June 13, 2011

Just because I'm chained
to the fence doesn't mean
I can't bark at the cars.

As Elka Ostrovsky in *Hot in Cleveland*,
Season 1, Episode 8

Well, now, do you prefer
being called Margaret or
Satan's mistress? We've
heard it both ways. Actually,
we've heard it lots of ways.

As Grandma Annie in *The Proposal*, 2009

The truth is I'm a great driver, but sometimes I like to drive real slow, just to mess with people.

As Elka Ostrovsky in *Hot in Cleveland*, Season 1, Episode 3

It's like we say in St. Olaf—
Christmas without fruitcake
is like St. Sigmund's Day
without the headless boy.

As Rose Nylund in *The Golden Girls*,
Season 5, Episode 12

I thought you wore too much makeup and were a slut. I was wrong. You don't wear too much makeup.

As Rose Nylund in *The Golden Girls*,
Season 3, Episode 15

I know I look square, but I'm like my father's tractor. I take a while to warm up, but once I get going, I can turn your topsoil till the cows come home.

As Rose Nylund in *The Golden Girls*, Season 1, Episode 5

You know what they say: You can lead a herring to water, but you have to walk really fast or he'll die.

As Rose Nylund in *The Golden Girls*, Season 2, Episode 7

Dorothy, was Sophia naked just now or does her dress really need ironing?

As Rose Nylund in *The Golden Girls*, Season 3, Episode 13

I'm a health nut. My favorite food is hot dogs with French fries. And my exercise: I have a two-story house and a very bad memory, so I'm up and down those stairs.

New York Times' TimesTalks event,
October 18, 2012

Naked Dogs

Hollywood restaurant Pink's Hot Dogs honored Betty in 2010 by creating "The Betty White Naked Dog," served exactly as she likes them: no condiments and no toppings.

66

I'm not a big cook. I only go in the kitchen to feed my dog.

99

Bon Appétit magazine, April 2, 2014

> My muffin hasn't had a cherry since 1939.

As Florence Dusty on *Saturday Night Live*,
Season 35, Episode 21

We didn't have Facebook
in my day, we had a phone
book, but you wouldn't
waste an afternoon on it.

Monologue on *Saturday Night Live*,
Season 35, Episode 21

SNL

On May 8, 2010, at the age of 88, Betty White became the oldest person to ever host *Saturday Night Live* after a grassroots Facebook campaign gathered so much attention that producer Lorne Michaels was persuaded to make it happen—the appearance garnered Betty her fifth primetime Emmy.

Well, I mean, if a joke or humor is bawdy, it's got to be funny enough to warrant it. You can't just have it bawdy or dirty just for the sake of being that—it's got to be funny.

Huffington Post, June 12, 2012

I like double entendre because
then the people who get it enjoy
it, and the people who don't
get it don't know about it.

National Public Radio, May 8, 2011

"

Humor is like music. It's a rhythm, and you just kind of get the rhythm of it, and you have to know not to let the beat go too long, but to leave a beat in there for it to gel, you know.

"

World of Pop Culture magazine, January 8, 2013

If you call me a comedian, I will be very grateful. I will thank you profoundly . . . It's fun once in a while to do a serious part but I really enjoy doing comedy because I love to laugh.

Sydney Morning Herald, July 16, 2012

CHAPTER
THREE

SHOW
BUSINESS

A pioneer of television with a showbiz
career spanning over 80 years, Betty
shares her insights on acting, the
audience, and working in Tinseltown.

It is important that you not believe your own publicity. Be grateful for whatever praise you receive but take it with a grain of salt.

If You Ask Me (And of Course You Won't), 2011

I am still, to this day, starstruck.
I look out at this audience and I
see so many famous faces, but
what really boggles my mind
is that I actually know many of
you. And I've worked with quite
a few . . . maybe had a couple.
And you know who you are.

Screen Actors Guild's Lifetime Achievement Award
acceptance speech, 2009

I just want to bring as much natural as I can. I'm not saying that people who take acting lessons are false. They're much better than I am, but it doesn't work for me.

Insider, January 17, 2021

"

Having a live audience makes a world of difference to the acting. It keeps your timing sharp. When something doesn't work, the actor can sense the reaction from the audience and quickly move on.

"

Wall Street Journal, May 4, 2007

So much of the humor on new sitcoms plays to the lowest common denominator. Wit isn't nearly given as much attention as slipping on a banana peel.

Wall Street Journal, May 4, 2007

66

The best kind of comedy
is the least self-conscious.
I think you just sort of let
the comedy happen without
the elbow nudge, 'Did you
get it? Did you get it?' I love
straight-face comedy or subtle,
relatively subtle, comedy.

99

Lena Lamoray interview, March 20, 2012

Do your work, learn your lines, and come in prepared. Don't think you can wing it, because you can't. We're in show business, which is fun, but take your business seriously, because it is a serious business.

Parade magazine, January 5, 2018

I cannot stand the people who get wonderful starts in show business and who abuse it . . . They are the most blessed people in the world, and they don't appreciate it.

Daily Mail, April 7, 2011

66

I started when television first started. I did the first broadcast that was ever done in Los Angeles. And television at that point was such a novelty . . . the big novelty was the fact that these people [the actors] were in your room with you.

99

Lena Lamoray interview, March 20, 2012

A Quartet of Bettys

There were four *The Betty White Shows*. The first was Betty's own radio program in the 1940s. She then launched her NBC variety TV show in 1954. Two further followed in 1958 on ABC and in 1977 on CBS.

The audience today has heard every joke. They know every plot . . . It's much more competitive now, because the audience is so much more— I want to say sophisticated.

Newsweek, January 17, 2020

Well, I think I've been around so long that they kind of think, well, she's always here so we might as well watch her.

On her younger audience, National Public Radio, May 8, 2011

I've learned that actors are just a part of the process; it's all about the writing. *Golden Girls* was pure gold: Once I read that script and saw the casting, I knew I had to be involved.

Hollywood Reporter, January 21, 2010

> **"**
>
> Professionalism. It's not about you, it's about everyone. Don't take yourself too seriously. Come to the set prepared and don't act like you know more than anyone else or you're more important than anyone else . . .
>
> **"**

On the most important thing she's learned,
Hollywood Reporter, January 21, 2010

Doing drama is, in a sense, easier. In doing comedy, if you don't get that laugh, there's something wrong.

IMDb.com

It's been phenomenal, but everybody keeps congratulating me on my resurgence and my big comeback. I haven't been away, guys. I've been working steadily for the last 63 years.

Today, NBC, December 20, 2010

I didn't choose to have
children because I'm focused
on my career. And I just don't
think, as compulsive as I am,
that I could manage both.

Sunday Morning with Katie Couric,
CBS, June 4, 2012

I just don't think you can do both: try to have a baby career and raise it and have a baby baby and raise it. And to try to do justice to either one. It was a very conscious decision on my part not to have children— which I have never regretted.

IMDb.com

"

. . . you can fool everybody else maybe that you know, but you can't fool that camera. That camera will know when you're faking it every time.

"

World of Pop Culture magazine,
January 8, 2013

I'm in the acting business.
That's the ego business.
When you get offers, the way
things are going now, you've
gotta enjoy it . . . appreciate
it and make the most of it.

IMDb.com

Being in show business is like living in a small town. People greet you like neighbors, not like strangers. And through the mail you form friendships that last for years, with people you've never even met.

Screen Actors Guild's Lifetime Achievement Award acceptance speech, 2009

Fun and Games

Due to her numerous appearances on such game shows as *Password*, *Hollywood Squares*, *What's My Line?*, *To Tell the Truth*, *Match Game*, and *Pyramid*, Betty has become known as the "First Lady of Game Shows."

If you get into a Broadway show and it doesn't work, you're a failure. And if it does work, you may be stuck for who knows how long. It just doesn't sound great to me!

If You Ask Me (And of Course You Won't), 2011

I'm blessed with learning easily.
I've always had a good thing
about memorizing quickly, and
I just leave the script kind of
open somewhere, and as I walk
by, I'll just take a swipe at it and
then go on about my business
and pretty soon it sticks.

Morefamousquotes.com

Throughout my career, I've always portrayed characters that were humorous, but also weren't afraid to speak their minds, especially when it came to racy or controversial topics. I think this struck a chord with the LGBT community.

Frontiers L.A., via *The Advocate*, October 10, 2011

If you have one good series, you know, it's a blessing. Two good series is unusual. Three is a phenomenon, but right now, I'm working with these wonderful women on *Hot in Cleveland* and . . . it's like the buddy-ship we had on *The Golden Girls* and *Mary Tyler Moore*.

Sunday Morning with Katie Couric, CBS, June 4, 2012

. . . when I started in 1950, most of the comedy shows were built around the man and then the woman filled in the family places or the girlfriend or whatever. But it didn't take long you know. Once you open the door to girls, they take over. You know how that goes.

In *Carol Burnett: A Woman of Character*,
PBS, 2007

Parades

A national treasure, Betty also loves a nationally broadcast parade. Between 1962 and 1972, Betty hosted Macy's Thanksgiving Day Parade alongside *Bonanza*'s Lorne Greene. She also spent 20 years as a color commentator for the annual Tournament of Roses Parade.

66

I just laugh. Have I
got them fooled.

99

On being referred to as a legend on the
Joy Behar Show, CNN, July 6, 2010

"

I had no idea that I would still be around at this point for one thing, but that I'd still be privileged enough to still be in this business. And it is such a privilege. And the bottom line I think to the television business is that unless you're a real bad egg, it is such fun. It really is.

"

Lifetime Achievement Award acceptance speech, Daytime Emmy Awards, 2015

CHAPTER
FOUR

WOMEN & ROMANCE

An early trailblazer for women in TV,
Betty never let anything hold her back.
She keeps alive her lust for life . . .
and men, especially her all-time
crush, Robert Redford.

I have no idea what color my hair is, and I never intend to find out.

If You Ask Me (And of Course You Won't), 2011

Butterflies are like women—
we may look pretty and
delicate, but we can fly
through a hurricane.

Screenrant.com, January 21, 2020

"

Oh I think that a big misconception was that you can't be funny and beautiful and smart. You got to pick one, but you can't have the whole package.

"

In *Carol Burnett: A Woman of Character*, PBS, 2007

Life with Betty

A pioneer in television, Betty was one of the first women to have full creative control of her own TV show (*Life with Elizabeth*), which she co-created, produced, and starred in while still living at home with her parents.

"

If a guy's a cutie, you've got to tap that booty.

"

As Elka Ostrovsky in *Hot in Cleveland*,
Season 2, Episode 20

66

I hate to admit it, but he melts my Häagen-Dazs.

99

As Rose Nylund in *The Golden Girls*,
Season 2, Episode 14

Does desire melt away with age?
I'm waiting for that day to come.

AARP The Magazine, November/December 2010

In my head I am the ultimate cougar. Animal lover that I am.

Piers Morgan Tonight, CNN,
April 17, 2012

"
I'm not what you might
call sexy, but I'm romantic.
Let's put it that way.
"

IMDb.com

I've always liked older men.
They're just more attractive
to me. Of course, at my age
there aren't that many left!

Parade magazine, October 31, 2010

66

I've enjoyed the opposite sex a lot. Always have. Always will.

99

Parade magazine, October 31, 2010

Of course, nobody's tearing my door down. If you're successful you're going to intimidate and scare off the people you'd like to spend time with. They're not going to approach you. And the ones who do are often there because you are a celebrity.

IMDb.com

Men are a hobby of mine. They might not know it though.

People magazine, November 24, 2016

66

Sex is pretty funny, let's face it. And the more seriously we take ourselves, the funnier sex gets, I think.

99

Uproxx.com, January 6, 2012

Whether you are a woman or you love one, you should remember that she's more than just flesh and bone.

ABC News, February 25, 2019

> 66
>
> I married my first husband
> because we wanted to
> sleep together. It lasted
> six months and we were
> in bed for six months.
>
> 99

AARP The Magazine, November/December 2010

Stars in Hollywood

Married for 18 "wonderful" years, Betty initially turned down her husband Allen's proposal but regretted losing that year she said no. Their stars on Hollywood's Walk of Fame are side by side.

66

Once you've had the best, who needs the rest?

99

When asked whether she would remarry,
Larry King Live, CNN, March 17, 2010

66

Remarry? No. Fool around?
Sure.

99

To Katie Couric, Yahoo! News, January 17, 2017

Well, it's been my experience that people who talk about it a lot don't do it very often.

About sex, as Rose Nylund in *The Golden Girls*, Season 2, Episode 23

My answer to anything under the sun, like, 'What have you not done in the business that you've always wanted to do?' is 'Robert Redford.'

Parade magazine, January 17, 2021

The hottest man in Hollywood
remains Robert Redford.
I've never met the man,
but I just enjoy fantasizing
about him completely!

Parade magazine, January 17, 2021

I still like to see that a man opens the door. I like those touches of chivalry that are fast disappearing. If I sound old-fashioned, it's because I'm as old as I am! But it's just polite.

Sydney Morning Herald, May 17, 2011

A lady likes to be complimented on her looks, her eyes, her figure. But the personality comments are much appreciated.

Daily Herald (Utah), May 13, 2011

CHAPTER
FIVE

CATS, DOGS . . .
& ELEPHANTS

A devoted animal advocate, Betty's love
affair with pets and wildlife led her to
promote more responsibility and
kindness toward her special friends.

66

Animals don't lie. Animals
don't criticize. If animals have
moody days, they handle them
better than humans do.

99

If You Ask Me (And of Course You Won't), 2011

During the Depression, my dad made radios to sell to make extra money. Nobody had any money to buy the radios, so he would trade them for dogs. He built kennels in the backyard, and he cared for the dogs.

If You Ask Me (And of Course You Won't), 2011

If everyone took personal responsibility for their animals, we wouldn't have a lot of the animal problems that we do. I'm a big spay-and-neuter supporter. Don't have babies if you're not going to take care of those babies.

New York Post, January 18, 2021

It's a little-known fact that one in three family pets gets lost during its lifetime, and approximately nine million pets enter shelters each year.

Wall Street Journal, October 2, 2012

I always wanted to be a zookeeper when I was growing up, and I've wound up a zookeeper! . . . my life is divided absolutely in half—half animals and half show business. You can't ask for better than two things you love the most.

TV Guide, November 11, 2009

I'm not into animal rights. I'm only into animal welfare and health. I've been with the Morris Animal Foundation since the '70s . . . I've worked with the L.A. Zoo for about the same length of time. I get my animal fixes!

IMDb.com

"

I stayed in show business to pay for my animal business.

"

Female.com.au

66

You can always tell about
somebody by the way they
put their hands on an animal.

99

AZQuotes.com

Animals are near and dear to my heart and I've devoted my life to trying to improve theirs.

Huffington Post, December 6, 2017

I love children. The only problem with children: They grow up to be people, and I just like animals more than I like people. It's that simple.

Entertainment Tonight, January 20, 2015

66

People who don't like cats
haven't been around them.
There's the old joke: Dogs
have masters, cats have staff.

99

AZQuotes.com

> **"**
> It was a thrill to be with Mr. Obama, but the big thrill was being with Bo, their dog. He's the cutest guy you've ever seen in your life.
> **"**

Huffington Post, June 12, 2012

To me there isn't an animal on the planet that I don't find fascinating and want to learn more about.

The Smithsonian magazine, May 14, 2012

When I am around animals, I don't pay attention to people.

Wall Street Journal, October 2, 2012

"

All creatures must learn to coexist. That's why the brown bear and the field mouse can share their lives in harmony. Of course, they can't mate or the mice would explode.

"

As Rose Nylund in *The Golden Girls*,
Season 5, Episode 5

I have my golden retriever now, Pontiac. He's a career-change guide dog from Guide Dogs for the Blind.

New York Daily News, June 16, 2009

A lot of people go, 'Well, I'll get a dog because I have a kid and a kid needs a dog.' And it doesn't work out for that dog and the dog is on the street.

IMDb.com

I just don't know how I would have lived without animals around me. I'm fascinated by them—both domestic pets and the wild community. They just are the most interesting things in the world to me . . .

AZQuotes.com

Once someone has the good fortune to share a true love affair with a golden retriever, one's life and one's outlook is never quite the same.

AZQuotes.com

Not so much the great apes, but monkeys. Elephants have a lovely sense of humor, too.

On which animals have the best sense of humor, *The Smithsonian* magazine, May 14, 2012

People forget what zoos do. If it weren't for zoos, we would have so many species that would be extinct today.

NBC News, November 22, 2011

66

Wilderness is harder and harder to find these days on this beautiful planet, and we're abusing our planet to the point of almost no return.

99

IMDb.com

"

Because I'm a patron of the [L.A.] zoo, I have backstage privileges with contact elephants. I go walking with my buddy Gita and the keeper. No chains. No nothing . . . I say, 'Trunk up, Gita,' and when I slap her tongue [it's like Gita is saying], 'Oh, she speaks my language.'

"

TimeGoesBy.net interview, June 30, 2011

Pet Care

A passionate campaigner for animal welfare and an honorary doctor of humane veterinary sciences, Betty turned down a role on *As Good as It Gets* because a scene shows Jack Nicholson's character pitching a small pet dog down a garbage chute.

CHAPTER
SIX

AGING
(DIS)GRACEFULLY

Betty was pivotal in portraying the
vibrant lives of senior women in the
groundbreaking *The Golden Girls* and,
in doing so, became a cultural icon
for all generations.

So you may not be as fast on your feet, and the image in your mirror may be a little disappointing, but if you are still functioning and not in pain, gratitude should be the name of the game.

If You Ask Me (And of Course You Won't), 2011

Gravity has taken over. So there's not much I can do about it . . . My problem with plastic surgery is you'll go to a women's press conference, or something like that, and old friends will come up and I kind of don't recognize them.

Joy Behar Show, CNN, July 6, 2010

I have no regrets at all. None.
I consider myself to be the
luckiest old broad on two feet.

Guinness World Records, September 4, 2013

World Record

For her 80-plus years in show business, Betty was awarded a Guinness World Record title for the Longest TV Career for an Entertainer (Female), first in 2014 and then winning it every year since.

> **"**
>
> I'm smokin' hot in the world.
> I'm still a golden girl. I may be a
> senior, so what . . . I'm still hot.
>
> **"**

Betty sings alongside electro artist Luciana
in the "I'm Still Hot" music video, released in
Ocotober 2011

"

I don't want to fight old age, but I am not going to invite it to live in either.

"

Betty White in Person, 1987

66

I'm a teenager trapped
in an old body.

99

Parade magazine, January 17, 2021

I hate wrinkles. On my face.
On my body. In my clothes.

Betty White in Person, 1987

Schedule a nightly appointment with Dr. Johnnie Walker.

On secrets to a long life, *The Late Show with David Letterman*, June 13, 2011

'Growing old' is a contradiction
in terms. Wouldn't it be
better to grow smart?

Betty White in Person, 1987

I don't seem to require a lot of sleep. I just—if I get four, five good hours, I'm fine. But sleeping is sort of dull. There's a lot of other good stuff that you can do without just lying down and closing your eyes.

Piers Morgan Tonight, CNN,
April 17, 2012

66

Oh, I don't need sleep. I just went to my hotel and had a cold hot dog and a vodka on the rocks.

New York magazine, May 14, 2010

I think it's your mental attitude.
So many of us start dreading
age in high school and that's
a waste of a lovely life.
 'Oh . . . I'm 30, oh, I'm 40,
oh, 50.' Make the most of it.

Huffington Post, May 24, 2011

I do mental exercises. I don't have any trouble memorizing lines because of the crossword puzzles I do every day to keep my mind a little limber.

ABC News, May 23, 2011

Can't an old person take
a nap without everyone
making a fuss about it?

As Annie Eason in *Annie's Point*, 2005

"

Exercise. Or don't.
What do I care?

"

The Late Show with David Letterman,
June 13, 2011

Since I am turning 99, I can
stay up as late as I want
without asking permission.

Associated Press News, January 16, 2021

My philosophy for staying young is [to] act bubbly every day. Drink bubbly every birthday!

Mentalfloss.com, January 17, 2019

66

You don't fall off the planet
once you pass a given age
. . . You don't lose any of your
sense of humor. You don't lose
any of your zest for life, or
your lust for life, if you will.

99

Today, NBC, 1991, re-aired August 7, 2015

"

Retirement is not in my vocabulary. They aren't going to get rid of me that way.

"

USA Today, January 21, 2010

Honors

Betty's won eight Emmy
awards, three Screen
Actors Guild awards, three
American Comedy Awards,
and a Grammy. She even
holds the record for the
longest span between Emmy
nominations—60 years
between her first in 1951
and her most recent in 2011.

Why retire from something if you're loving it so much and enjoying it so much . . . What would I do with myself?

Huffington Post, November 12, 2013

My mother always used to say, 'The older you get, the better you get. Unless you're a banana.'

As Rose Nylund in *The Golden Girls*, Season 2, Episode 16

People say, 'But Betty, Facebook is a great way to connect with old friends.' Well, at my age, if I want to connect with old friends I need a Ouija board.

Monologue on *Saturday Night Live*, Season 35, Episode 21

I don't go around thinking
'Oh, I'm 90, I better do this or
I better do that.' I'm just Betty.
I'm the same Betty that I've
always been. Take it or leave it.

The Guardian, November 10, 2012

I think I've been spoiled enough, don't you think? Might as well quit while I'm ahead! But I'm not going to quit, that's for sure.

Huffington Post, June 12, 2012

Now that I'm 91, as opposed
to being 90, I'm much wiser.
I'm much more aware,
and I'm much sexier.

Betty White's Second Annual 90th Birthday Special,
NBC, February 5, 2013

Older women still have a full life. Maybe writers don't address it these days, but it doesn't change the facts.

Associated Press, September 15, 2010

I inherited some wonderful, good genes from my mother and dad. So being blessed with good health gives you the strength, and loving what you do—is a privilege that keeps you going.

Daily Actor, April 24, 2012

One thing they don't tell you about growing old—you don't feel old, you just feel like yourself. And it's true. I don't feel 89 years old. I simply am 89 years old.

If You Ask Me (And of Course You Won't), 2011

Kindness and consideration of somebody besides yourself.
I think that keeps you feeling young. I really do.

Sunday Morning with Katie Couric,
CBS, June 4, 2012

"

Don't try to be young. Just open your mind. Stay interested in stuff. There are so many things I won't live long enough to find out about, but I'm still curious about them.

"

IMDb.com

It's amazing—past a certain age, you can get away with murder. You can do anything and people will say, 'Well, the poor old soul, she's . . . you know . . . '

Harper's Bazaar, March 31, 2014

66

Well the sun sets every night
but I just won't go away.

99

Entertainment Tonight, January 20, 2015

Warmly. I hope they remember something funny. I hope they remember a laugh.

On how she wants to be remembered,
Parade magazine, January 5, 2018